This Journal Belongs To:

_____

How To Use This Journal?

The five daily questions (four for the morning and one at night) are designed to;
- Help you focus so you can feel more prepared, be more productive and achieve your goals faster.
- Let go of any negative emotions that might be holding you back or self sabotaging thoughts that interfere with your day and hold you back.
- Feel more gratitude and positivity every day.

Doing this daily practice of setting your intentions for the day will help you act as your "best self" and achieve more.

Take a look at your pages every two weeks (or monthly) and see if you notice any repeated behaviours or thoughts that you either want to stop or encourage. This will help you focus on the important stuff in your life, not just the urgent.

1. Eliminate Distractions. You deserve at least two minutes to yourself daily no matter how busy you are!
2. Do it before anything else - no screens, no shower, optional caffeine!
3. Have no filter - this is your time and space to be honest and express yourself.
4. Don't think too much - just note down what's on your mind without any judgement.
5. Prepare the night before with the journal by your bed or at a spot you go to first thing in the morning with a pen or pencil ready.

Morning:

I am grateful for…

I will let go of…

I will progress in my goals today by focusing on…

What one thing can I do for myself that would make me feel really good today?

Night:

What was the most challenging thing about today and what can I do to avoid repeating this experience in my life?

Morning:

I am grateful for…

I will let go of…

I will progress in my goals today by focusing on…

What one thing can I do for myself that would make me feel really good today?

Night:

What was the most challenging thing about today and what can I do to avoid repeating this experience in my life?

Morning:

I am grateful for…

I will let go of…

I will progress in my goals today by focusing on…

What one thing can I do for myself that would make me feel really good today?

Night:

What was the most challenging thing about today and what can I do to avoid repeating this experience in my life?

Morning:

I am grateful for…

_____

_____

I will let go of…

_____

_____

I will progress in my goals today by focusing on…

_____

_____

What one thing can I do for myself that would make me feel really good today?

_____

_____

Night:

What was the most challenging thing about today and what can I do to avoid repeating this experience in my life?

_____

_____

_____

Morning:

I am grateful for…

I will let go of…

I will progress in my goals today by focusing on…

What one thing can I do for myself that would make me feel really good today?

Night:

What was the most challenging thing about today and what can I do to avoid repeating this experience in my life?

Morning:

I am grateful for…

I will let go of…

I will progress in my goals today by focusing on…

What one thing can I do for myself that would make me feel really good today?

Night:

What was the most challenging thing about today and what can I do to avoid repeating this experience in my life?

Morning:

I am grateful for…

I will let go of…

I will progress in my goals today by focusing on…

What one thing can I do for myself that would make me feel really good today?

Night:

What was the most challenging thing about today and what can I do to avoid repeating this experience in my life?

Morning:

I am grateful for…

I will let go of…

I will progress in my goals today by focusing on…

What one thing can I do for myself that would make me feel really good today?

Night:

What was the most challenging thing about today and what can I do to avoid repeating this experience in my life?

Morning:

I am grateful for…

I will let go of…

I will progress in my goals today by focusing on…

What one thing can I do for myself that would make me feel really good today?

Night:

What was the most challenging thing about today and what can I do to avoid repeating this experience in my life?

Morning:

I am grateful for…

_____

_____

I will let go of…

_____

_____

I will progress in my goals today by focusing on…

_____

_____

What one thing can I do for myself that would make me feel really good today?

_____

_____

Night:

What was the most challenging thing about today and what can I do to avoid repeating this experience in my life?

_____

_____

_____

_____

Morning:

I am grateful for…

I will let go of…

I will progress in my goals today by focusing on…

What one thing can I do for myself that would make me feel really good today?

Night:

What was the most challenging thing about today and what can I do to avoid repeating this experience in my life?

Morning:

I am grateful for…

I will let go of…

I will progress in my goals today by focusing on…

What one thing can I do for myself that would make me feel really good today?

Night:

What was the most challenging thing about today and what can I do to avoid repeating this experience in my life?

Morning:

I am grateful for…

I will let go of…

I will progress in my goals today by focusing on…

What one thing can I do for myself that would make me feel really good today?

Night:

What was the most challenging thing about today and what can I do to avoid repeating this experience in my life?

Morning:

I am grateful for…

I will let go of…

I will progress in my goals today by focusing on…

What one thing can I do for myself that would make me feel really good today?

Night:

What was the most challenging thing about today and what can I do to avoid repeating this experience in my life?

Morning:

I am grateful for…

I will let go of…

I will progress in my goals today by focusing on…

What one thing can I do for myself that would make me feel really good today?

Night:

What was the most challenging thing about today and what can I do to avoid repeating this experience in my life?

Morning:

I am grateful for…

_____

_____

I will let go of…

_____

_____

I will progress in my goals today by focusing on…

_____

_____

What one thing can I do for myself that would make me feel really good today?

_____

_____

Night:

What was the most challenging thing about today and what can I do to avoid repeating this experience in my life?

_____

_____

_____

_____

Morning:

I am grateful for…

I will let go of…

I will progress in my goals today by focusing on…

What one thing can I do for myself that would make me feel really good today?

Night:

What was the most challenging thing about today and what can I do to avoid repeating this experience in my life?

Morning:

I am grateful for…

I will let go of…

I will progress in my goals today by focusing on…

What one thing can I do for myself that would make me feel really good today?

Night:

What was the most challenging thing about today and what can I do to avoid repeating this experience in my life?

Morning:

I am grateful for…

I will let go of…

I will progress in my goals today by focusing on…

What one thing can I do for myself that would make me feel really good today?

Night:

What was the most challenging thing about today and what can I do to avoid repeating this experience in my life?

Morning:

I am grateful for…

I will let go of…

I will progress in my goals today by focusing on…

What one thing can I do for myself that would make me feel really good today?

Night:

What was the most challenging thing about today and what can I do to avoid repeating this experience in my life?

Morning:

I am grateful for…

I will let go of…

I will progress in my goals today by focusing on…

What one thing can I do for myself that would make me feel really good today?

Night:

What was the most challenging thing about today and what can I do to avoid repeating this experience in my life?

Morning:

I am grateful for…

I will let go of…

I will progress in my goals today by focusing on…

What one thing can I do for myself that would make me feel really good today?

Night:

What was the most challenging thing about today and what can I do to avoid repeating this experience in my life?

Morning:

I am grateful for…

I will let go of…

I will progress in my goals today by focusing on…

What one thing can I do for myself that would make me feel really good today?

Night:

What was the most challenging thing about today and what can I do to avoid repeating this experience in my life?

Morning:

I am grateful for…

I will let go of…

I will progress in my goals today by focusing on…

What one thing can I do for myself that would make me feel really good today?

Night:

What was the most challenging thing about today and what can I do to avoid repeating this experience in my life?

Morning:

I am grateful for…

I will let go of…

I will progress in my goals today by focusing on…

What one thing can I do for myself that would make me feel really good today?

Night:

What was the most challenging thing about today and what can I do to avoid repeating this experience in my life?

Morning:

I am grateful for…

I will let go of…

I will progress in my goals today by focusing on…

What one thing can I do for myself that would make me feel really good today?

Night:

What was the most challenging thing about today and what can I do to avoid repeating this experience in my life?

Morning:

I am grateful for…

I will let go of…

I will progress in my goals today by focusing on…

What one thing can I do for myself that would make me feel really good today?

Night:

What was the most challenging thing about today and what can I do to avoid repeating this experience in my life?

Morning:

I am grateful for…

_____

_____

I will let go of…

_____

_____

I will progress in my goals today by focusing on…

_____

_____

What one thing can I do for myself that would make me feel really good today?

_____

_____

Night:

What was the most challenging thing about today and what can I do to avoid repeating this experience in my life?

_____

_____

_____

Morning:

I am grateful for…

I will let go of…

I will progress in my goals today by focusing on…

What one thing can I do for myself that would make me feel really good today?

Night:

What was the most challenging thing about today and what can I do to avoid repeating this experience in my life?

Morning:

I am grateful for…

I will let go of…

I will progress in my goals today by focusing on…

What one thing can I do for myself that would make me feel really good today?

Night:

What was the most challenging thing about today and what can I do to avoid repeating this experience in my life?

Morning:

I am grateful for…

I will let go of…

I will progress in my goals today by focusing on…

What one thing can I do for myself that would make me feel really good today?

Night:

What was the most challenging thing about today and what can I do to avoid repeating this experience in my life?

Morning:

I am grateful for…

I will let go of…

I will progress in my goals today by focusing on…

What one thing can I do for myself that would make me feel really good today?

Night:

What was the most challenging thing about today and what can I do to avoid repeating this experience in my life?

Morning:

I am grateful for…

I will let go of…

I will progress in my goals today by focusing on…

What one thing can I do for myself that would make me feel really good today?

Night:

What was the most challenging thing about today and what can I do to avoid repeating this experience in my life?

Morning:

I am grateful for…

I will let go of…

I will progress in my goals today by focusing on…

What one thing can I do for myself that would make me feel really good today?

Night:

What was the most challenging thing about today and what can I do to avoid repeating this experience in my life?

Morning:

I am grateful for…

I will let go of…

I will progress in my goals today by focusing on…

What one thing can I do for myself that would make me feel really good today?

Night:

What was the most challenging thing about today and what can I do to avoid repeating this experience in my life?

Morning:

I am grateful for…

I will let go of…

I will progress in my goals today by focusing on…

What one thing can I do for myself that would make me feel really good today?

Night:

What was the most challenging thing about today and what can I do to avoid repeating this experience in my life?

Morning:

I am grateful for…

I will let go of…

I will progress in my goals today by focusing on…

What one thing can I do for myself that would make me feel really good today?

Night:

What was the most challenging thing about today and what can I do to avoid repeating this experience in my life?

Morning:

I am grateful for…

I will let go of…

I will progress in my goals today by focusing on…

What one thing can I do for myself that would make me feel really good today?

Night:

What was the most challenging thing about today and what can I do to avoid repeating this experience in my life?

Morning:

I am grateful for…

I will let go of…

I will progress in my goals today by focusing on…

What one thing can I do for myself that would make me feel really good today?

Night:

What was the most challenging thing about today and what can I do to avoid repeating this experience in my life?

Morning:

I am grateful for…

I will let go of…

I will progress in my goals today by focusing on…

What one thing can I do for myself that would make me feel really good today?

Night:

What was the most challenging thing about today and what can I do to avoid repeating this experience in my life?

Morning:

I am grateful for…

I will let go of…

I will progress in my goals today by focusing on…

What one thing can I do for myself that would make me feel really good today?

Night:

What was the most challenging thing about today and what can I do to avoid repeating this experience in my life?

Morning:

I am grateful for…

I will let go of…

I will progress in my goals today by focusing on…

What one thing can I do for myself that would make me feel really good today?

Night:

What was the most challenging thing about today and what can I do to avoid repeating this experience in my life?

Morning:

I am grateful for…

I will let go of…

I will progress in my goals today by focusing on…

What one thing can I do for myself that would make me feel really good today?

Night:

What was the most challenging thing about today and what can I do to avoid repeating this experience in my life?

Morning:

I am grateful for…

I will let go of…

I will progress in my goals today by focusing on…

What one thing can I do for myself that would make me feel really good today?

Night:

What was the most challenging thing about today and what can I do to avoid repeating this experience in my life?

Morning:

I am grateful for…

I will let go of…

I will progress in my goals today by focusing on…

What one thing can I do for myself that would make me feel really good today?

Night:

What was the most challenging thing about today and what can I do to avoid repeating this experience in my life?

Morning:

I am grateful for…

I will let go of…

I will progress in my goals today by focusing on…

What one thing can I do for myself that would make me feel really good today?

Night:

What was the most challenging thing about today and what can I do to avoid repeating this experience in my life?

Morning:

I am grateful for…

I will let go of…

I will progress in my goals today by focusing on…

What one thing can I do for myself that would make me feel really good today?

Night:

What was the most challenging thing about today and what can I do to avoid repeating this experience in my life?

Morning:

I am grateful for…

_____

_____

I will let go of…

_____

_____

I will progress in my goals today by focusing on…

_____

_____

What one thing can I do for myself that would make me feel really good today?

_____

_____

Night:

What was the most challenging thing about today and what can I do to avoid repeating this experience in my life?

_____

_____

_____

Morning:

I am grateful for…

I will let go of…

I will progress in my goals today by focusing on…

What one thing can I do for myself that would make me feel really good today?

Night:

What was the most challenging thing about today and what can I do to avoid repeating this experience in my life?

Morning:

I am grateful for…

I will let go of…

I will progress in my goals today by focusing on…

What one thing can I do for myself that would make me feel really good today?

Night:

What was the most challenging thing about today and what can I do to avoid repeating this experience in my life?

Morning:

I am grateful for…

I will let go of…

I will progress in my goals today by focusing on…

What one thing can I do for myself that would make me feel really good today?

Night:

What was the most challenging thing about today and what can I do to avoid repeating this experience in my life?

Morning:

I am grateful for…

I will let go of…

I will progress in my goals today by focusing on…

What one thing can I do for myself that would make me feel really good today?

Night:

What was the most challenging thing about today and what can I do to avoid repeating this experience in my life?

Morning:

I am grateful for…

I will let go of…

I will progress in my goals today by focusing on…

What one thing can I do for myself that would make me feel really good today?

Night:

What was the most challenging thing about today and what can I do to avoid repeating this experience in my life?

Morning:

I am grateful for…

I will let go of…

I will progress in my goals today by focusing on…

What one thing can I do for myself that would make me feel really good today?

Night:

What was the most challenging thing about today and what can I do to avoid repeating this experience in my life?

Morning:

I am grateful for…

I will let go of…

I will progress in my goals today by focusing on…

What one thing can I do for myself that would make me feel really good today?

Night:

What was the most challenging thing about today and what can I do to avoid repeating this experience in my life?

Morning:

I am grateful for…

I will let go of…

I will progress in my goals today by focusing on…

What one thing can I do for myself that would make me feel really good today?

Night:

What was the most challenging thing about today and what can I do to avoid repeating this experience in my life?

Morning:

I am grateful for…

I will let go of…

I will progress in my goals today by focusing on…

What one thing can I do for myself that would make me feel really good today?

Night:

What was the most challenging thing about today and what can I do to avoid repeating this experience in my life?

Morning:

I am grateful for…

I will let go of…

I will progress in my goals today by focusing on…

What one thing can I do for myself that would make me feel really good today?

Night:

What was the most challenging thing about today and what can I do to avoid repeating this experience in my life?

Morning:

I am grateful for…

I will let go of…

I will progress in my goals today by focusing on…

What one thing can I do for myself that would make me feel really good today?

Night:

What was the most challenging thing about today and what can I do to avoid repeating this experience in my life?

Morning:

I am grateful for…

I will let go of…

I will progress in my goals today by focusing on…

What one thing can I do for myself that would make me feel really good today?

Night:

What was the most challenging thing about today and what can I do to avoid repeating this experience in my life?

Morning:

I am grateful for…

I will let go of…

I will progress in my goals today by focusing on…

What one thing can I do for myself that would make me feel really good today?

Night:

What was the most challenging thing about today and what can I do to avoid repeating this experience in my life?

Morning:

I am grateful for…

I will let go of…

I will progress in my goals today by focusing on…

What one thing can I do for myself that would make me feel really good today?

Night:

What was the most challenging thing about today and what can I do to avoid repeating this experience in my life?

Morning:

I am grateful for…

I will let go of…

I will progress in my goals today by focusing on…

What one thing can I do for myself that would make me feel really good today?

Night:

What was the most challenging thing about today and what can I do to avoid repeating this experience in my life?

Morning:

I am grateful for…

I will let go of…

I will progress in my goals today by focusing on…

What one thing can I do for myself that would make me feel really good today?

Night:

What was the most challenging thing about today and what can I do to avoid repeating this experience in my life?

Morning:

I am grateful for…

I will let go of…

I will progress in my goals today by focusing on…

What one thing can I do for myself that would make me feel really good today?

Night:

What was the most challenging thing about today and what can I do to avoid repeating this experience in my life?

Morning:

I am grateful for…

I will let go of…

I will progress in my goals today by focusing on…

What one thing can I do for myself that would make me feel really good today?

Night:

What was the most challenging thing about today and what can I do to avoid repeating this experience in my life?

Morning:

I am grateful for…

I will let go of…

I will progress in my goals today by focusing on…

What one thing can I do for myself that would make me feel really good today?

Night:

What was the most challenging thing about today and what can I do to avoid repeating this experience in my life?

Morning:

I am grateful for…

I will let go of…

I will progress in my goals today by focusing on…

What one thing can I do for myself that would make me feel really good today?

Night:

What was the most challenging thing about today and what can I do to avoid repeating this experience in my life?

Morning:

I am grateful for…

I will let go of…

I will progress in my goals today by focusing on…

What one thing can I do for myself that would make me feel really good today?

Night:

What was the most challenging thing about today and what can I do to avoid repeating this experience in my life?

Morning:

I am grateful for…

I will let go of…

I will progress in my goals today by focusing on…

What one thing can I do for myself that would make me feel really good today?

Night:

What was the most challenging thing about today and what can I do to avoid repeating this experience in my life?

Morning:

I am grateful for…

I will let go of…

I will progress in my goals today by focusing on…

What one thing can I do for myself that would make me feel really good today?

Night:

What was the most challenging thing about today and what can I do to avoid repeating this experience in my life?

Morning:

I am grateful for…

I will let go of…

I will progress in my goals today by focusing on…

What one thing can I do for myself that would make me feel really good today?

Night:

What was the most challenging thing about today and what can I do to avoid repeating this experience in my life?

Morning:

I am grateful for…

I will let go of…

I will progress in my goals today by focusing on…

What one thing can I do for myself that would make me feel really good today?

Night:

What was the most challenging thing about today and what can I do to avoid repeating this experience in my life?

Morning:

I am grateful for…

I will let go of…

I will progress in my goals today by focusing on…

What one thing can I do for myself that would make me feel really good today?

Night:

What was the most challenging thing about today and what can I do to avoid repeating this experience in my life?

Morning:

I am grateful for…

I will let go of…

I will progress in my goals today by focusing on…

What one thing can I do for myself that would make me feel really good today?

Night:

What was the most challenging thing about today and what can I do to avoid repeating this experience in my life?

Morning:

I am grateful for…

I will let go of…

I will progress in my goals today by focusing on…

What one thing can I do for myself that would make me feel really good today?

Night:

What was the most challenging thing about today and what can I do to avoid repeating this experience in my life?

Morning:

I am grateful for…

I will let go of…

I will progress in my goals today by focusing on…

What one thing can I do for myself that would make me feel really good today?

Night:

What was the most challenging thing about today and what can I do to avoid repeating this experience in my life?

Morning:

I am grateful for…

I will let go of…

I will progress in my goals today by focusing on…

What one thing can I do for myself that would make me feel really good today?

Night:

What was the most challenging thing about today and what can I do to avoid repeating this experience in my life?

Morning:

I am grateful for…

I will let go of…

I will progress in my goals today by focusing on…

What one thing can I do for myself that would make me feel really good today?

Night:

What was the most challenging thing about today and what can I do to avoid repeating this experience in my life?

Morning:

I am grateful for…

I will let go of…

I will progress in my goals today by focusing on…

What one thing can I do for myself that would make me feel really good today?

Night:

What was the most challenging thing about today and what can I do to avoid repeating this experience in my life?

Morning:

I am grateful for…

I will let go of…

I will progress in my goals today by focusing on…

What one thing can I do for myself that would make me feel really good today?

Night:

What was the most challenging thing about today and what can I do to avoid repeating this experience in my life?

Morning:

I am grateful for…

I will let go of…

I will progress in my goals today by focusing on…

What one thing can I do for myself that would make me feel really good today?

Night:

What was the most challenging thing about today and what can I do to avoid repeating this experience in my life?

Morning:

I am grateful for…

I will let go of…

I will progress in my goals today by focusing on…

What one thing can I do for myself that would make me feel really good today?

Night:

What was the most challenging thing about today and what can I do to avoid repeating this experience in my life?

Morning:

I am grateful for…

I will let go of…

I will progress in my goals today by focusing on…

What one thing can I do for myself that would make me feel really good today?

Night:

What was the most challenging thing about today and what can I do to avoid repeating this experience in my life?

Morning:

I am grateful for…

I will let go of…

I will progress in my goals today by focusing on…

What one thing can I do for myself that would make me feel really good today?

Night:

What was the most challenging thing about today and what can I do to avoid repeating this experience in my life?

Morning:

I am grateful for…

_____

_____

I will let go of…

_____

_____

I will progress in my goals today by focusing on…

_____

_____

What one thing can I do for myself that would make me feel really good today?

_____

_____

Night:

What was the most challenging thing about today and what can I do to avoid repeating this experience in my life?

_____

_____

_____

Morning:

I am grateful for…

I will let go of…

I will progress in my goals today by focusing on…

What one thing can I do for myself that would make me feel really good today?

Night:

What was the most challenging thing about today and what can I do to avoid repeating this experience in my life?

Morning:

I am grateful for…

I will let go of…

I will progress in my goals today by focusing on…

What one thing can I do for myself that would make me feel really good today?

Night:

What was the most challenging thing about today and what can I do to avoid repeating this experience in my life?

Morning:

I am grateful for…

I will let go of…

I will progress in my goals today by focusing on…

What one thing can I do for myself that would make me feel really good today?

Night:

What was the most challenging thing about today and what can I do to avoid repeating this experience in my life?

Morning:

I am grateful for…

I will let go of…

I will progress in my goals today by focusing on…

What one thing can I do for myself that would make me feel really good today?

Night:

What was the most challenging thing about today and what can I do to avoid repeating this experience in my life?

Morning:

I am grateful for…

I will let go of…

I will progress in my goals today by focusing on…

What one thing can I do for myself that would make me feel really good today?

Night:

What was the most challenging thing about today and what can I do to avoid repeating this experience in my life?

Morning:

I am grateful for…

I will let go of…

I will progress in my goals today by focusing on…

What one thing can I do for myself that would make me feel really good today?

Night:

What was the most challenging thing about today and what can I do to avoid repeating this experience in my life?

Morning:

I am grateful for…

I will let go of…

I will progress in my goals today by focusing on…

What one thing can I do for myself that would make me feel really good today?

Night:

What was the most challenging thing about today and what can I do to avoid repeating this experience in my life?

Morning:

I am grateful for…

I will let go of…

I will progress in my goals today by focusing on…

What one thing can I do for myself that would make me feel really good today?

Night:

What was the most challenging thing about today and what can I do to avoid repeating this experience in my life?

Morning:

I am grateful for…

I will let go of…

I will progress in my goals today by focusing on…

What one thing can I do for myself that would make me feel really good today?

Night:

What was the most challenging thing about today and what can I do to avoid repeating this experience in my life?

Morning:

I am grateful for…

I will let go of…

I will progress in my goals today by focusing on…

What one thing can I do for myself that would make me feel really good today?

Night:

What was the most challenging thing about today and what can I do to avoid repeating this experience in my life?

Morning:

I am grateful for…

I will let go of…

I will progress in my goals today by focusing on…

What one thing can I do for myself that would make me feel really good today?

Night:

What was the most challenging thing about today and what can I do to avoid repeating this experience in my life?

Morning:

I am grateful for…

I will let go of…

I will progress in my goals today by focusing on…

What one thing can I do for myself that would make me feel really good today?

Night:

What was the most challenging thing about today and what can I do to avoid repeating this experience in my life?

Morning:

I am grateful for…

I will let go of…

I will progress in my goals today by focusing on…

What one thing can I do for myself that would make me feel really good today?

Night:

What was the most challenging thing about today and what can I do to avoid repeating this experience in my life?

Morning:

I am grateful for…

I will let go of…

I will progress in my goals today by focusing on…

What one thing can I do for myself that would make me feel really good today?

Night:

What was the most challenging thing about today and what can I do to avoid repeating this experience in my life?

Morning:

I am grateful for…

_____

_____

I will let go of…

_____

_____

I will progress in my goals today by focusing on…

_____

_____

What one thing can I do for myself that would make me feel really good today?

_____

_____

Night:

What was the most challenging thing about today and what can I do to avoid repeating this experience in my life?

_____

_____

_____

Notes

Notes

We hope you loved using your

Two Minute Morning Journal

and that it has been useful in helping you live as your best self, achieve more and let go of any reoccurring negative thoughts or behaviours in your life.

Please take a moment to leave a review on amazon and if you'd like to continue this daily practice click on our author name to see other fun and stylish cover styles we publish in this series.

Made in the USA
Columbia, SC
14 November 2021

48948352R00059